Teaching Obedience

A RESOURCE FOR PARENTS WHO WISH TO
LAY THE RIGHT FOUNDATION FOR BRINGING
UP THEIR CHILDREN IN THE LORD

Dr. Walt Brock

The Ironwood Family Toolbook Series

God's first institution, the family, is under attack more than ever! The Christian home is bombarded with immoral entertainment, deceitful philosophy, and humanistic education. The need for core, biblical values is the defense for such warfare. The Family Toolbook Series is designed to equip fathers, mothers, pastors, counselors, or teachers that serve families in the church or school setting by giving them practical guides to formulating a biblical foundation for life. This series covers fundamental truths that when applied become tools God can use to change lives.

Copyright 2005 by Walt Brock
ISBN 1-931787-15-8
LOC 2005926531

Unless otherwise noted, Scripture quotations are from the
Authorized King James Version.

For information concerning the Ironwood Family Toolbook Series or any other resources listed in this book, contact us at www.ironwood.org.

Managing Editor, Shannon B. Steuerwald
Cover Design, Susanna I. Capetz
Content Layout, Allison Pust

Iron Sharpeneth Iron Publications
Newberry Springs, California

Table of Contents

Foreword

There is absolutely no doubt in my mind that without my wonderful wife Betty—the helper God created for me and designed for us both to work and play in tandem—my life would have been hollow and empty. I could not have written this book, or had the experiential background necessary to do so without her being beside me and involved in the process. So I want to take this opportunity to say thank you to her, and to let everyone in the world know how much I love and cherish her. My darlin' Betty, I love you so…

I also want to thank our children, who are all adults today and are all serving in various ministry capacities. I want to thank them for allowing me to use them as illustrations not only here, but in other forums as well. I want to thank them for making Betty and me joyful parents and grand-parents as we see them going about the busy life of ministry and/or parenthood. It has been a real joy seeing them bring up their own children in the nurture and admonition of the Lord. The biblical phrase found in *Deuteronomy 6* of teaching "their sons and their son's sons" has taken on real meaning and relevance in this life (and also I might add, a reward for all the diligence necessary in those years of discipline). As Betty and I observe our children, we often praise the Lord for His grace and mercy. No matter what we did right or wrong in our children's upbringing, they still have a free will; and thus, we must give God all the glory and credit. To God be the glory because first, it is all of His grace; and second, it is all of His grace; and third, success would have been impossible without His grace.

So, to our children, Mom and I both thank you for the joy you have brought into our lives. May God bless each of you and your families, abundantly as you continue on in life and in ministry. We love you so…

Ephesians 6:3—That it may be well with thee, and thou mayest live long on the earth.

Deuteronomy 6:2—That thou mightest fear the LORD thy God, to keep all his statutes and his commandments, which I command thee, thou, and thy son, and thy son's son, all the days of thy life; and that thy days may be prolonged.

Thanks,

Walt

Chapter One
Teaching Children to Obey

Submitting yourselves one to another
in the fear of God. Ephesians 5:21

Writing about discipline is always easier than actually doing the work of disciplining. Disciplining can be painful work. Learning personally to become a disciplined person is often difficult, not to mention the toil involved in helping others to become disciplined in their lives. The pain is not always physical pain; there is the mental and emotional pain that comes from carefully doing things in the right order and sequence or from exchanging that which is good and enjoyable for that which is more important. Sometimes repetition, effort, loneliness, denial, or lack of time can also make the process heartrending. Discipline is a treasure of great value, and the diligent quest for it will not be accomplished without experiencing some pain.

I once overheard one of my mentors in life recommend to a group of students that they read *The Disciplined Life* by Richard S. Taylor. He said it was a classic and one of the half-dozen or so books that he had read that actually changed his life. Well, if my mentor thought that much of this book, I determined to get a copy and read it. So I went out and bought a copy. Not wanting to spend all the time necessary to read this short book all the way through, I decided to skip over most of the book and read the section in the last chapter entitled "How to Become a Disciplined Person." What do you suppose I found when I turned to that chapter? The first section had a subtitle that said "No Shortcuts!" followed by the first paragraph. I expected a real key thought here, but all I found was this statement:

> "Begin by reading the entire book through, including the introduction, if you have not already done so. Some of you will spot the title of this chapter while scanning the table of contents and, recognizing that becoming a disciplined person is the goal; will suppose that to read only this chapter will be sufficient. Such an attempt may be symptomatic of your need of discipline" (page 81).

Talk about getting it right between the eyes. Needless to say, I went back and read the whole book. But "no shortcuts" is what I remember most about that book.

The same lesson must be learned by every parent who desires for his child to be able to claim God's promise concerning obedience:

> Children, obey your parents in the Lord: for this is right. Honor thy father and mother; which is the first commandment with promise; **that it may be well with thee, and thou mayest live long on the earth.** (*Ephesians 6:1–3*)

There are truly no shortcuts to the end goal of bringing up disciplined children; but one key element may appear to be, by itself, a shortcut. In this case, appearances can be deceiving; for this shortcut only works well in conjunction with the whole process. Yet without this key element, the whole process can often unravel.

So, let us get the shortcut out of the way so that we can then go back and do the real work of learning how to have happy, loving children in our homes. I urge parents to keep in mind that while the shortcut is a key factor in teaching children to obey, and that by using it alone one could achieve some semblance of outward success, there is much more to discipline than this shortcut. Yet without it, a parent is almost helpless in the face of a demanding child.

I call the shortcut the *D Factor* with the "D" standing for *dominance*. Anyone who has grown up on a ranch, a farm, or around many children understands the *D Factor*, even if he has not thought about it in this way before. Every flock of chickens, herd of horses, or group of children will have what many have called a "pecking order." Within the group there is an unwritten order of who can peck who and who can or cannot peck others. That pecking order is built on the principle of dominance. Sometimes the strongest will dominate; but more often, one who is weaker will dominate the stronger. In a herd of horses, a rather old mare will often dominate. With a flock of chickens, determining a pattern is harder; but observation will reveal that one chicken in the pen can and will peck every other chicken, and then another will peck every other chicken except number one. And so it goes through the flock, until one poor old chicken never pecks another but gets pecked by all. She lives a life full of fear and fleeing. She is frazzled, nervous, and skinny. She will often die much before her peers. She has no *D Factor* while the one at the top has the most *D Factor* in the flock.

A parent needs to understand that when his child was born into the world, he possessed a certain *D Factor* level; and experience will either feed it, starve it, or tame it. If a parent wants his child to obey him, he must have a personal *D Factor* greater than the child's. The parent must be very careful not only with controlling his own *D Factor* but also with the feeding of the child's *D Factor*, because selfishness is a monster whose appetite can become insatiable. I have seen young toddlers absolutely dominate their parents. Mom and Dad are completely oblivious to their bondage and yet are so frazzled and harried that they have little energy left to enjoy each other or their growing family.

According to the Bible (*Ephesians 6:1*), if a child wins this battle of the will, he really loses. The Scripture requires parents to command their children. Parents must determine (make a decision) that they will have a stronger *D Factor*, although a controlled one, than their children do. Simply stating the apparent shortcut, parents must decide to be in control and determine that they will not allow their children to usurp that God-given responsibility of being the ones in charge. Children quickly learn if and how far they can push against the boundaries. Each decision parents make in response to their children's pushing tells the children to stop or push farther. Consistency of follow through is vital since children learn by a very early age their parents' *D Factor* level and use that knowledge accordingly. Applying this shortcut to parenting is crucial, but good discipline requires much more.

Chapter Two
Discipline in the Bible

Children, obey your parents in the Lord: for this is right.
Honor thy father and mother; (which is the first
commandment with promise;) that it may be well with thee,
and thou mayest live long on the earth. And, ye fathers,
provoke not your children to wrath: but bring them
up in the nurture and admonition of the Lord. Ephesians 6:1–4

Discipline is more than just punishment. This truth goes contrary to many opinions; but without a total view of discipline, we cannot hope to achieve the final results parents so desperately desire. In spite of what we have just said, no real shortcut to our desired end product exists; one must go through the whole process in order to achieve the real desired product. Let's start with the biblical definition of discipline and then see how it can be implemented in a family. For this discussion, we will turn to the cornerstone passage of Scripture, *Ephesians 6:1–4*, that deals with the upbringing of children (see above).

This passage addresses both the children and the parents. Each bears some responsibility in the final outcome of a child's bringing up process. The parents have their responsibility; the children have theirs. What one does or does not do has no absolute control over what the other does

> Although parents have a great deal of influence over their child, they have no absolute control over their child's will.

or does not do. No biblical formula guarantees that if the parents do *a*, *b*, and *c*, then *x* will happen. No formula for parental action will ever disengage the will of children. God created man with a free will; and although God desires that all men everywhere be saved, each person is individually responsible to respond correctly to the gospel and by faith believe on the Lord Jesus Christ. Without each person's participation in the process by his acceptance or receiving of Jesus Christ, there will be no salvation. In much the same way, the child in the Christian home must decide to submit his will to his parents and learn from their teaching and example. In the end, the grown child will be held responsible as to whether he chooses the right way or the wrong way. Although parents have a great deal of influence over their children, they have no absolute control over their will.

As a parent, I know how much I dearly wanted to find some magic formula that would guarantee that my children would make the right choices in life. Many times parents go to the extreme of being super controlling of their children, dominating every aspect of their lives and making all their choices with the hope that those choices will result in those children turning out right. That extreme is as bad as *laissez-faire* parents who allow their children to do whatever they want with the mistaken notion that all people have a spark of good in them that will eventually come out if left to their own devices.

By early adulthood, both extremes will often result in these children having raging self-wills bent on doing whatever pleases themselves. They have learned to completely ignore their parents and their God. Neither extreme produces children who will honor their parents, and neither will receive the promised blessing from God, "that it may be well with thee, and thou mayest live long on the earth." Failure to find such a magic formula should not leave the parent without hope. The lack of magic formulas just underscores the importance of finding and staying within the biblical balance found in fulfilling the parents' responsibility of bringing up their children.

Although this Ephesians passage mentions parents and fathers and mothers, parenting responsibilities can confidently be applied to both parents or to those legally responsible for the children in their formative years, as children growing up in their grandparents' home or as step-children. Fathers represent the corporate head of the home, but in many cases, certain responsible adults who have the legal and moral obligation to bring up children should do so with the assurance that they have the biblical authority to do so.

Both parents are given the responsibility of bringing up their children, but the order of Scripture for the Christian home is always with the leadership of the husband lovingly guiding his family in a God-honoring manner. Thus, while the father should take the lead, both parents must be actively involved in the proper discipline, training, and teaching of the children that God has given them.

Provoking to Anger

Ephesians 6:4 also addresses an important command—"fathers, provoke not your children to wrath." Although we are not dealing with the subject of anger in detail in this book, parents must clearly understand that bringing up a child in such a way that generates a deep, seething attitude of hostility within him colors everything red in the child's world. As a whole, our society is angry. Evidence of such is very vivid in the news with many incidents of road rage, workplace violence, school and domestic violence, and aggression being reported all across our nation. For the most part, these acts are driven by the boiling-over emotion of anger.

The Bible gives us a clear warning of the danger of anger just by observing the company anger keeps in the following lists:

Let all bitterness, and **wrath**, and **anger**, and clamour, and evil speaking, be put away from you, with all malice. (*Ephesians 4:31*)

Now the works of the flesh are manifest, which are these; Adultery, fornication, uncleanness, lasciviousness, idolatry, witchcraft, hatred, variance, emulations, **wrath**, strife, seditions, heresies, envyings, murders, drunkenness, revellings, and such like: of the which I tell you before, as I have also told you in time past, that they which do such things shall not inherit the kingdom of God. (*Galatians 5:19–21*)

But now ye also put off all these; **anger**, **wrath**, malice, blasphemy, filthy communication out of your mouth. Lie not one to another, seeing that ye have put off the old man with his deeds. (*Colossians 3:8–9*)

A quick look at a concordance reveals 230 times in Scripture where the word *anger* is used and 198 times where the word *wrath* is used. Fifty-two of those times, the two words are used in the same verse. The Bible

14

clearly teaches that the detrimental affects of a deep, seething hostility creates an attitude of life. I have included a short Bible study in the appendix of this book for further study.

Another passage of Scripture that speaks directly to this subject of parents causing an angry spirit in their children is *Colossians 3:21*: "Fathers, provoke not your children to *anger*, lest they be discouraged." Unreasonableness, harshness, as well as verbal and physical expressions of anger provoke children and thus discourage them. The word *discouraged* is used only this once in the Scriptures and *Strong's* defines it as being "disheartened, dispirited, broken in spirit";[1] however, *Vine's*, by looking at the root words, adds to that a "negative spirit…denoting feeling, passion; hence Eng., fume."[2] Going one step further, *Webster's 1828 Dictionary* defines *fume* as, "To be in a rage; to be hot with anger. He frets, he fumes, he stares, he stamps the ground." Parents who provoke their children can, by their attitudes and actions, kindle a harmful character trait and lessen their children's quality of life.

Bring Them Up

Bringing up children clearly indicates a process which will not be accomplished without a long and faithful diligence to fulfill the responsibility. *Strong's* says *bring up* simply means "to nourish up to maturity, to nourish."[3] Another word dictionary defines *bring up* as "to nourish, rear…to bring up to maturity such as children…in the sense of to train or educate,"[4] continuing on to say that a synonym might mean "to shepherd or take general care of." *Webster's* says that *nourish* means to "feed and cause to grow… to educate; to instruct; to promote growth in attainments." Just like there is more to harvesting a good crop of oranges than just planting the seed and coming back later to pick the fruit, there is more to child rearing than just having a baby and making sure the college bills are paid. Children require much time, care, and labor between birth and adulthood.

So, if parents desire to bring up their children to maturity, they must mentally prepare themselves for the long haul with each stage or phase in their children's lives building on top of the previous stage. The first stage, learning to submit to one's God-given authority, is best learned in the home. Maybe that is why the first of the Ten Commandments dealing with man's relationship to his fellow man tells us to honor our father and mother. Maybe that is also why there seems to be a connection between learning to submit as a child and salvation as is found in the book of Proverbs.

> Withhold not correction from the child: for if thou beatest him with the rod, he shall not die. Thou shalt beat him with the rod, and shalt deliver his soul from hell. (*Proverbs 23:13–14*)

God commands all men everywhere to be saved (*1 Timothy 2:4*), and that command requires a humbling of one's self and obedience to God in placing one's faith in the Lord and accepting Him as his Savior.

> **Bringing up children clearly indicates a process which will not be accomplished without a long and faithful diligence to fulfill the responsibility.**

Teaching children to obey has eternal consequences which go far beyond just making life easier for the parents during their child-rearing years. No

16

doubt life will be made easier, but the parental motive here is obedience to God, and the payoff for the long process of bringing them up could be eternal for their children.

Nurture

The word *discipline* was not a word in common usage when the King James Version of the Bible was translated. In fact, the word *discipline* is only found one time in our English King James Version in *Job 36:3*: "He [God] openeth also their ear to discipline." If this verse is an insight into how God works, and it is, parents should be praying that God would give their children a disposition to obey. Another word from the ancient languages and found in the New Testament, *paideia*, will help us understand the biblical concept of discipline. Strong's concordance dictionary defines *paideia* as follows:

"...the whole training and education of children (which relates to the cultivation of mind and morals, and employs for this purpose now commands and admonitions, now reproof and punishment). It also includes the training and care of the body."[5]

Paideia is translated in three different ways in the New Testament: *nurture* in *Ephesians 6:4*, *instruction* in *2 Timothy 3:16*, and *chastening* in *Hebrews 12:5, 7–9, 11*. All three translations are from the same Greek word, yet each translation gives us a different aspect of what discipline is all about. True biblical training is a combination of all three.

Nurture addresses the aspect of discipline that involves training as a long process using a variety of methods including giving commands, holding accountable, reproving when wrong, and administering punishment, if necessary. While this type of training of the mind, morals, and behavior of children is basically training by act, it nevertheless tends toward harshness without being accompanied by teaching, which is why in another context it is translated as "instruction in righteousness."

Instruction is the aspect of discipline that targets the increasing of virtue. Seeing the context in which it is used in *2 Timothy 3:16*, "All scripture is given by inspiration of God, and is profitable for doctrine, for reproof, for correction, for instruction in righteousness," helps us gain some insight into its use in the home. Instruction is preceded by:

Doctrine, which is teaching the truth (how to do it)

Reproof, which is identifying deviation from the truth (how one is doing it wrong)

Correction, which is teaching by word and example the true way (how to do it right)

Instruction in righteousness, which is training in the self-disciplined habit of proper behavior (how to keep doing right)

Trying to accomplish the last one, instruction in righteousness, without laying down the foundation of the first three is one of the ways parents provoke their children to anger.

Chastening or *chastisement* is the third necessary aspect of discipline and the one that many people identify as the only aspect of discipline. It involves pain and punishment; oftentimes with young children, it takes the form of spanking. However, if spanking is a parent's only tool of chastisement, he is not following the pattern of chastisement given to us by our Savior. The parent definitely has a variety of methods of chastisement besides physical pain. On the other hand, parents do their children an injustice if they follow the modern-day philosophy of the world that all spanking is automatically wrong and that it teaches children violence. Two things must be remembered about chastisement:

1. **Chastisement's motivation must be right.**

   The motivation of chastisement must be love. The Lord gives us the pattern in *Revelation 3:19:* "As many as I love, I rebuke and chasten: be zealous therefore, and repent."

2. **Chastisement's goal must be right.**

   The goal of chastisement must be improvement, growth, or change. If the aim is only to inflict pain or to release some of a parent's own frustration, then the spanking is wrong to administer. The goal of this type of discipline is not simply punishment; to think that is to confuse the goal with the method.

Parents must not administer chastisement unless they have themselves under control with the wellbeing and good of the child as their goal. This command of God must be carried out very carefully in love. A few years ago I watched a young mother deal with her preschool son concerning his misbehavior in church. She marched him out with threatening words of a spanking; she marched him back in with the ultimatum that he better never embarrass her again. As I watched the young boy sit obediently throughout the rest of the service, my heart went out to this young mother who had in just a few moments taught her son that his chastisement was for her selfish benefit and not because of her love for him and his future. She had won the battle on that Sunday morning, but the war would probably be lost if she continued with the same motivation and goal.

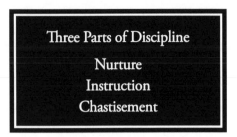

Three Parts of Discipline

Nurture
Instruction
Chastisement

Nurture then is primarily disciplining by act, but it must include some aspect of teaching by word and example to be effective.

Admonition

Admonition, on the other hand, is the aspect of discipline that involves teaching by word and by example; but it must include some action. The Greek word from which we get the word admonish is *nouthesia*, literally meaning "a putting in mind ... to warn ... and is used in *Ephesians 6:4* of that which is ministered by the Lord."[6] *Nouthesia* is the training by word, whether of encouragement, or, if necessary, by reproof or remonstrance. But it is more than just remonstrance or reproof. "Admonition differs from remonstrance, in that the former is warning based on instruction; the latter may be little more than expostulation. For example, though Eli remonstrated with his sons, (*1 Samuel 2:24*), he failed to admonish them" (*1 Samuel 3:13*).[7] Parents often believe that they have taught by word just because they have given reproof when a child disobeys or reasons with a child concerning his disobedience. When a parent reasons with his child concerning the impropriety of the child's conduct, he has attained only a small part of admonition.

If we understand admonition correctly, its focus is not merely obedience in action, but its focus is also in the heart and the will of the child. You have probably heard of the child who was spanked by his father for not obeying when he was told to get up off the floor and sit in the chair. He said to his father, "Okay, I'll sit in the chair, but in my heart I'm still on the floor." While that child may have obeyed outwardly, there was no real obedience until he submitted in his heart as well. In the end, obedience boils down to three simple truths: (1) the child must know what is required, (2) the child must submit to what is required, and (3) the child must do what is required.

Admonition plays a key role in two of those three aspects of obedience. It is through admonition that complete information is given on the how and the why of the command, and it is through admonition that the intellect and the will are influenced to submit. There are, of course, times when there is no time to teach; safety demands instant obedience. But instant obedience in such circumstances is much more likely if the general tone of bringing up the children is practiced with using both the discipline by act (nurture) and discipline by word (admonition) in combination as the Lord intended. The real goal of admonition is not an isolated act of obedience but an overall change in the child, predisposing him to obedience time after time without a constant tug of war going on. To ignore admonition is to doom oneself to constantly fight the same battle over and over again. The type of admonition parents use with their children will change as the children grow older and

> **An obedient child must**
> - **Know what is required**
> - **Submit to what is required**
> - **Do what is required**

become wiser, but even toddlers can perceive some admonition when properly given.

Admonition may take the form of verbal and hands-on instruction, evaluative teaching on how to do it better, praise for doing right, or some other way of getting through to the mind with words of wisdom and instruction. Sometimes it takes the form of a warning, a reminder, an encouragement, or a correction. As children grow closer to independence, admonition gets closer to the form of advice parents would wisely and carefully use as their children establish their own homes.

Deuteronomy 6:7, one of the key Old Testament passages dealing with teaching our children, tells parents to teach their children *diligently*, which in this passage means "to pierce or penetrate."[8] As parents, we must figure out how to teach so that the message gets through "thick skulls" so that our children really hear and learn what is being taught. The old proverb, "If the student has not learned, the teacher has not taught," speaks of the challenge to parents to teach the lessons of life so that their children really do get it.

Parents must also remember that there is a qualifier on admonition as it is used in *Ephesians 6:4*—the admonitions must be of the Lord. Admonition is used here as a responsibility of parents to teach their children in a systematic way all about the Lord and His ways. The end result should be that children have a respect for the Word of God and view it as the source of all truth and as the foundation for their lives. An example of this is found in the New Testament: "Now all these things happened unto them for ensamples: and they are written for our admonition, upon whom the ends of the world are come" (*1 Corinthians*

10:11). In this passage, we are commanded to admonish others by using the failures of the children of Israel as examples as they suffered the consequences of their disobedience. This is an example of using the mistakes and misdeeds of others as a teaching tool and not having to learn the lessons through personal experience.

The phrase "of the Lord" is also a qualifier for the term *nurture* or *discipline*. Discipline is administered as obedience to the Lord, obey-

> **To ignore admonition is to doom oneself to constantly fight the same battle over and over again.**

ing His command to do so, but only in a manner that will glorify Him. Discipline must be administered in such a way as to be pleasing to Him and consistent with all scriptural commands and admonitions regarding one's relationships with his fellow man. Unbalanced discipline administered in anger for the wrong purposes ends up being disobedience to God; and His angels are watching: "Take heed that ye despise not one of these little ones; for I say unto you, That in heaven their angels do always behold the face of my Father which is in heaven." (*Matthew 18:10*)

1. Strong, James. *Enhanced Strong's Lexicon.* Oak Harbor, WA: Logos Research Systems, Inc., 1995.

2. Vine, W. E. *Vine's Expository Dictionary of Old and New Testament Words,* s.v. "discouraged." Grand Rapids, MI: Fleming H. Revell, 1981.

3. Strong, *Enhanced Strong's Lexicon.*

4. Strong, *Enhanced Strong's Lexicon.*

5. Strong, *Enhanced Strong's Lexicon*

6. Vine, *Vine's Expository Dictionary of Old and New Testament Words,* s.v "nouthesia."

7. Vine, *Vine's Expository Dictionary of Old and New Testament Words,* s.v "exercise."

8. Strong, *Enhanced Strong's Lexicon.*

Bringing Up Young Children

Ephesians 6:4

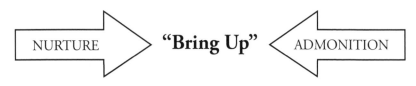

NURTURE   **"Bring Up"**   ADMONITION

Training

Paideia—The whole training and education of children as it relates to the cultivation of the mind and morals using commands, teaching, reproofs, and punishment. Showing how and being a good example are essential.

To nourish up to maturity, not just physically, but in all areas of life

Teaching

Teaching primarily, but not exclusively, by word. It includes exhortation, encouragement, teaching, remonstrance, reproof, or blame as required. It is an appeal to reason, but it may involve correction by deed if necessary.

Needs of Young Children

1. They need to know who is in control—*D factor.*
2. They need the joy and happiness of obedience.
3. They need the security of parental love for each other.
4. They need unconditional love—touch, time, talk, tone, total attention.
5. They need to know where the real boundary line is.
6. They need someone to shut down their manipulation.

Chapter Three
Chastisement of Children

If ye endure chastening, God dealeth with you as with sons; for what son is he whom the father chasteneth not? Hebrews 12:7

Chasten thy son while there is hope, and let not thy soul spare for his crying. Proverbs 19:18

In the last chapter, we talked briefly about the three aspects of discipline derived from the translation of the Greek word *paideia*. In this chapter, we will concentrate on one of those three aspects, the one that deals with punishment. I feel this deserves some concentrated attention, because "punishment" seems to be how people primarily define the concept of discipline. Their understanding is that an obedient child is a disciplined child and a disobedient child needs to be disciplined. Discipline involves much more than just punishment; and when parents do not understand the total concept, they have difficulty in realizing their goal of obedient children.

As Scripture teaches us in the verse above, chastisement is a tool of growth and development that God uses with His children (believers) and that He does indeed chastise them as evidence of their being part of God's family. In other words, this is a family matter reserved by God for use within the family, and the use of it is proof of unconditional family love within the family. "For whom the Lord loveth he chasteneth, and scourgeth every son whom he receiveth" (*Hebrews 12:6*). To fully understand the biblical concept of chastisement, we must look at it from two views: the view of action and the view of the destination or goal of chastisement.

The Action View

Three actions or methods are used in chastisement that describes what parents are doing to and with their children as they chastise them. *Vine's Dictionary* indicates that the verb form of *paideia* suggests that we must look at chastisement in the broad sense of the whole education, instruction, and training of our children. Therefore, as we focus on the methodology of chastisement, we must understand that it is still part of the overall process of bringing up our children in the Lord's way. *Vine's Dictionary* indicates that this action will take one of three forms:

1. Correcting by words, before and after
2. Correcting through the "infliction of evils and calamities"[1]
3. Correcting through the infliction of physical pain

We can find biblical examples how God has and is using all three of these methods with us as believers even today. As we take note of this, we should consider our chastisement of our children and how we would want God to deal with us if we should backslide or go astray from His revealed Word and will.

In the first methodology of using words to correct, parents should make sure that children have a clear expectation of what they are going to be held accountable for. Then when expectations are not fulfilled, the parent can proceed with questions and then to the old proverbial "lecture," ending with re-teaching the expectations and an encouragement to do better next time. Often times, when children desire to please their parents, this is all the chastisement that is necessary in order to correct behavior which will eventually form their character. However, if words should fail, the parent must move on to using one of the next two actions. These next two actions are not necessarily consecutive in nature, but rather two options from which to choose in order to deal with disobedience in an appropriate way.

With the second method, parents follow the example of God in manufacturing a result or consequence related to the wrongdoing. In the Old Testament (*2 Chronicles 20:36–37* and *1 Kings 22:48–50*), we find an incident where King Jehosaphat disobeyed the Lord by partnering with an unbelieving and evil king for the purpose of commerce. As a result God destroyed Jehosaphat's ships and his ability to do commerce. Jehosaphat learned His lesson and would not even let his men return in the same boats with those who hated God. This is an example of God withholding or removing something of value, yet related to the misdeed, for the purpose of correction. The closer the withheld item or privilege is to the misdeed, the more effective the corrective value of the chastisement. Children must be old enough to understand the connection between their wrong actions and the consequence inflicted.

The third method deals with the actual infliction of physical pain. Because we have another whole chapter of this book that deals with spankings, I will not dwell on it here; but it is an important part of the puzzle and must be used appropriately for God's promises to be fulfilled. A biblical example of this is found in the life of the apostle Paul. In *2 Corinthians 6:9–10*, he related that some of the events in his life that had caused him great pain and suffering were, in fact, chastening from the Lord. While the chastening temporarily brought him some suffering, the end result was always rejoicing. This aspect of correcting our children for the purpose of their long-term benefit is never pleasant, for either us or for them; but it is vitally necessary if parents and their grown children are going to enjoy their future together and rejoice in the Lord.

Neither of these last two actions is limited to one age group or the other; however, one is certainly suited better for one age than the other. Spanking is best used on children before puberty, and other manufactured consequences are best used on older children. Some blending of these methods is useful in the transition years, but the younger the child the less they understand the purpose of related consequences. That is why spanking is so effective for young children since they understand the message of stimulus and response long before they can even talk. Likewise, as the teens become older, the better they will understand related consequences and the more they will grow to resent spankings that increasingly seem to assault their personhood.

The Destination View

When our Lord said, "As many as I love, I rebuke and chasten: be zealous therefore, and repent" (*Revelation 3:19*), He was giving us His goal for the use of chastisement in the lives of believers: repent, turn back, change your ways, or just simply, obey! The purpose was for the good of the one being chastised, to get him back into the place of God's blessing. Thus, there is always a teaching factor in chastisement, and this is precisely the point a parent must always remember. Chastisement is never punishment just for the sake of punishment but is always part of the total package of acting in love for the best interests of the child. Just as every believer needs to learn to submit to the authority of God in his life, children need to learn to obey their parents. This learning of obedience to parents then becomes lessons for all believers on the necessity of submitting to the rule of God in their lives, both in childhood and adulthood.

Another place in Scripture where the word *chasten* is used is in *1 Corinthians 11:31–32*: "Now if we would judge ourselves, we should not be judged. But when we are judged, we are chastened of the Lord, that we should not be condemned with the world." The teaching here (v.32) is that chastening today is for the purpose of avoiding some future greater judgment,

> **Chastening today is for the purpose of avoiding some future greater judgment.**

which, in essence, is what we are trying to do with our children—chastise them for their disobedience today so they will obey us in the future and thus avoid an even greater tragedy in their lives. We teach a child to respond to our voice and obey us in little things like obeying the command to "stop running across the room and come to Daddy now." Then when we are in a parking lot and our young son starts running into a danger zone, he will stop at our command and return obediently to us, without our having to chase and grab him. There will come a time when a parent will not be able to physically dominate his child. At that point, when the only response is to the parent's voice, what will happen then? To the parent of a headstrong child who is out of control, this may seem like an unrealistic goal; but if these principles are consistently and lovingly put into practice at home, results will be evident out in public. The results will not occur overnight, for the child must be convinced that the parent means business. And periodical reminders will be necessary, whether in childhood, during puberty, or past puberty.

While teaching the child to obey our voice is a worthy goal, there is actually a better goal taught in verse 31, the goal of self-discipline. Self-discipline occurs when believers honestly judge and discipline themselves in obedience to the Scriptures (responding to the correction of words) so that God does not need to chasten them physically or circumstantially in order to get their attention and their repentance. For our children, this is the goal of learning to obey for the purpose of character development: the ability to do the right thing, at the right time, with the right attitude. The character trait of self-discipline does not just appear, but is a learned characteristic. It is learned in the school of chastisement for the purpose of obedience, which in turn will eventually, after much consistent and loving application, result in self-discipline in the lives of our children as they move into adulthood.

In conclusion, the godly chastisement of our children is administered in love and is motivated for the benefit of the person being disciplined, not the one administering the chastisement. The action of chastisement will take three forms: the form of teaching and corrective words, the form of manufactured consequences, or the form of a spanking. The ultimate goal revolves around each child personally learning self-discipline and obedience to the words of God. This is best accomplished when parents are loving (self-sacrificially doing the hard thing today) the future of their children (their children's adult life, their children's children, and the eternal future of all).

To understand and implement chastisement properly, we can refer to the following ten biblically-based principles.

1. Recognize that children are born with a sinful nature that operates at full strength from the beginning (*Psalm 51:5; 58:3*).

   Children will be selfish and sinful without any outside help. Some parents today try to isolate their children from the world and its sinful influences. For the most part, those efforts are commendable; but parents must never forget that children have born within them the seed of sin which will sprout and grow without any outside help. Parents need to help their children, through chastisement, to grow into Christ-likeness in their lives.

2. Realize your duty and authority as parents and remember that God holds you accountable for your responsibilities.

   Parents have the God-given responsibility

   • to train their children—*Proverbs 22:6*

   • to nurture (discipline) and admonish their children—
     Ephesians 6:4

   • to teach diligently (piercingly, so that they understand and get
     the message)—*Deuteronomy 6:6–7*

- to command their children—*Genesis 18:19*

- to impart and teach wisdom—*Proverbs 1–7*

- to live an exemplary life so their children will listen to their words—*Deuteronomy 6:10–21*

- to explain hard-to-understand things and to share the praises of God—*Psalm 78:1–4*

- to teach, to give verbal encouragement, to give responsibility—*1 Thessalonians 2:11*

- to not provoke anger in their children—*Colossians 3:21*

- and to chasten children for their good and future benefit—*Hebrews 12:5–11*

3. Record specific disciplinary goals you make for your children. Write them down and make realistic plans to accomplish those goals (*Genesis 18:19; Luke. 2:52; 1 Thessalonians 2:13; 2 Timothy 3:17*).

Parents should break down their goals and objectives for each child for each various age or stage of life. My wife and I found it helpful to periodically use trips away from the responsibilities of home and the children for this purpose. These trips were designed to have free time for us to discuss issues related to the children and our family without outside interference. Once goals are established, planning and organization to accomplish them must be decided upon and then put into motion. Then parents must evaluate the effectiveness of their actions and constantly make adjustments as necessary.

4. Reject ungodly and humanistic teachings prevalent in our society. Guard yourself and your children from such subtle attacks (*Colossians 2:8; 2 Timothy 3:1–9*).

The philosophy of the world is found in the newspaper, the advice of others, the media, the advertising world, and in education (public, Christian, or home). It is insidious and pervasive; no source outside the Bible (including this book) can be trusted as entirely free from the philosophy of the world and our enemy Satan. Constant vigilance is necessary. We must be constantly evaluating everything for the following philosophical errors:

*   Relativism—situation ethics, no absolutes; motivations and sincerity make a difference

*   Pluralism—tolerance; no right and wrong; only right

*   Secularism—no intervention by God; man can solve all the ills of society through education, society, and government…because man is basically good

*   Humanism—man is the measure of all things; self-esteem, self-actualization, and individual self-determinism; man has rights, and he can choose for himself without considering God's will

*   Materialism—things and money bring peace, happiness, and security

*   Pantheism—god is everywhere and in everything, including the environment and the animal world; there is a good force and an

evil force; find the good and follow it regardless of its source; all religions lead to the same place if one sincerely follows them

5. Research the specific needs of each child. Consider IQ, personality traits, spiritual gifts, and natural ability.

Parents need to think about each of their children. Each is an individual creation of God with differing physical and mental abilities, differing interests, differing learning skills and patterns, differing *D factors,* and differing ways of exhibiting them. Each will have a different personality and differing birth orders and experiences. Because of all these differences, parents do children great harm when they try to put them all in the same mold without thought of their differences, including considering their God-given spiritual gifts and His calling in their lives. Think about them and design an individual plan for each, for each is worth it! Fairness is not always equal *(Psalms 139:13–17, 23–24; Proverbs 22:6*—the way he should go = bent).

6. Remember that in order to discipline correctly, you must love your child and discipline for his future, not for self-centered motives.

Family love is never easy; it is self-sacrificial and unconditional. But children must be absolutely convinced of a parent's love. It helps to say it, but a parent must show it. It cannot be faked; they will know! *(Proverbs 13:24; 19:8; 29:17; Hebrews 12:5–11; Psalm 78:1–8; Titus 2:4)*

7. Reduce discipline to its lowest common denominator—obedience or disobedience *(Exodus 20:12; Colossians 3:20; Ephesians 6:1–2).*

34

Because a child's freewill submission to God is the goal of a parent's chastisement, put everything possible into this box. It is not just that they did not pick up the toys when you asked them to, it is that they disobeyed when they did not do what was commanded. Ask the question, "Are you going to obey?" as the last warning before a spanking.

8. Responsibly discipline early for the most effective results. Discipline should continue in a consistent but appropriate manner at each new age level as long as the child is in the home (*Psalm 53:3; 58:3; Proverbs 13:24; 19:18; 22:6; 23:13–14*).

   Many parents do not start disciplining early enough or keep it up long enough to insure that their children have every opportunity to properly learn the character trait of self-discipline. Several times, in relation to bringing up children, the Scriptures refer to the "process of time," so it is a long drawn-out affair, starting at birth and ending at independence. But by far the most important time in a child's life are those first few years when he needs to learn to obey, and the earlier the better. If older children have not yet learned this yet, teaching obedience becomes your starting point.

9. Reasonably administer a wise upbringing (balancing chastisement, instruction, and nurturing) without provoking your children to anger (*Ephesians 6:4*).

   Beyond the obvious things that provoke children to wrath such as inconsistency, insults, injustice, and integrity issues, parents need to discern the difference between childish foolishness and rebellion.

There is a big difference in essence, and there needs to be a difference in reaction and consequences between the ignorance of immaturity and the disobedience of stubbornness.

10. Rely on the rod of correction, by faith, knowing that it is God's way. Use it early, wisely, and carefully (*Proverbs 13:24; 22:15; 23:13–14*).

No one is suggesting that you hit your children, but the philosophers of this world will use loaded terminology like that to convince others of their opinion. It takes faith to believe that God knows what He is talking about in the Scriptures. It takes faith to begin spanking correctly, and it will take faith to continue. Do not settle for less than complete obedience, which will in the end blossom into a self-disciplined lifestyle for your children.

Parents know there is no joy in administering a spanking. Their joy comes with the results of proper discipline and is spoken of in the Scriptures as the "peaceable fruit of righteousness." Spankings are just part of the whole process and should never be considered as an act of discipline that stands alone. Proper and complete verbal teaching and training should always precede spanking.

Proverbs 10:13—In the lips of him that hath understanding wisdom is found: but a rod *is* for the back of him that is void of understanding.

- *Proverbs 13:24*—He that spareth his rod hateth his son: but he that loveth him chasteneth him quickly.

- *Proverbs 19:18*—Chasten thy son while there is hope, and let not thy soul spare for his crying.

- *Proverbs 22:15*—Foolishness *is* bound in the heart of a child; *but* the rod of correction shall drive it far from him.

- *Proverbs 23:13*—Withhold not correction from the child: for *if* thou beatest him with the rod, he shall not die.

- *Proverbs 23:14*—Thou shalt beat him with the rod, and shalt deliver his soul from hell.

- *Proverbs 29:15*—The rod and reproof give wisdom: but a child left *to himself* bringeth his mother to shame.

1. Vine, W. E. *Vine's Expository Dictionary of Old and New Testament Words,* s.v. "chastening." Grand Rapids, MI: Fleming H. Revell, 1981.

Chapter Four

The Four "D" Box:
Determining the Boundaries

*All we like sheep have gone astray, we have turned
every one to his own way. Isaiah 53:6a*

In order to teach obedience wisely, a parent must establish boundaries—first of all, in his own thinking. He should picture in his mind a box with four sides. When the child crosses the line to go outside this box, the action will automatically result in a spanking. The parent is now not deciding to spank the child; rather, the child is choosing a behavior that demands a spanking. As we were raising our children, Betty and I observed a variety of parents: some were inconsistent about what they were spanking for, others hardly ever or never spanked their children, and the third group seemed to spank their children for everything—big, little, and in between. I was probably most nervous about the third group whose children could only differentiate between offenses by how hard the spanking was. I felt most compassion for the inconsistent group and their first confused and then angry children trying to interpret the always shifting meaning of the discipline. The second group, those who rarely if ever spanked their children, saddened me by the lack of value they placed upon their children and their needed training.

I did not like to spank my children. I found it a very disagreeable and difficult task to perform. If I had not come to grips with the truth that this was God's method, I'd have probably shirked this responsibility. But I could not do so and be obedient to God in my child-rearing responsibilities. So my wife and I decided to determine from God's Word what warranted a spanking. We came up with four primary areas. Although each was capable of being exhibited in a variety of ways, we decided on four basic things for which we would spank our children.

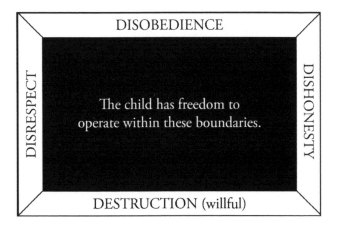

1. **Disobedience**—failure to obey a command given by the parents or those in authority over them.

2. **Disrespect**—failure to honor their mother and father. In the Ten Commandments, children are commanded by God to honor their parents. In essence, such respect will help form the basis of all future relations in their lives. If children get this one wrong, all of life will become a bag of worms.

3. **Destruction**—willful destruction of one's own property or the property of others. All things in life are a gift from God and should be respected as such. This can be an act of commission or omission.

4. **Dishonesty**—next to disobedience, the most destructive of character of the four behaviors. When God said that He hated six things, He actually listed seven, repeating lying. Dishonesty is something God really hates.

    Proverbs 6:16–19—These six things doth the LORD hate: yea, seven are an abomination unto him: A proud look, a **lying tongue,** and hands that shed innocent blood, An heart that deviseth wicked imaginations, feet that be swift in running to mischief, **A false witness that speaketh lies,** and he that soweth discord among brethren.

Teaching the Boundaries

Once parents have determined their boundaries, they must, through admonition, teach and clearly communicate those boundaries to their children. Once parents are sure the children understand the boundary, they can be free to spank the child for the offense of crossing the boundary. Parents must always give a clear warning as to when that was likely to occur. For instance, if Betty and I told one of our children to pick up his toys, and he kept fooling around—half way picking up the toys and half way doing his own thing, we would simply ask the question, "Are you going to obey Mommy (or Daddy)?" Without any shouting or yelling, that was the last thing the child heard before the spanking ceremony would begin. That question was a definite wake-up call to the child and was, in essence, a form of admonition in the form of a warning that judgment was coming. During the toddler years, that important question of "Are you going to obey?" simply trains the child that his choices determine the outcome. The use of the word obey is the key indicator until he is old enough to really understand the whole issue.

Children will ALWAYS test the boundaries!

There are three things to remember about this plan:

1. A parent can count on a child to push against any and every boundary he will ever draw. It is impossible to make the box so big that a child will never push against the line. In the garden of Eden, only one prohibition was given in the whole wide wonderful world; and Adam and Eve crossed it. A parent thinking that he can set his boundaries at some compromise position that both he and the child can live with is faulty reasoning. Wherever the line is, the child will push. He will check the parent's reaction, and then he will cross the line to see if the line is real. When he finds out it is, he finds security, and through such security finds contentment. If a child's world is without real discernible (for him) boundaries, that world is a very fearful and anxious place to be. The establishment and enforcement of boundaries is evidence of parents' love that is strong enough to pay attention and to care for the wellbeing of their children. Happy children are the result.

2. Consistency is absolutely essential for this plan to work, but consistency is easy when you only have four rules to remember. Granted, parents will need discernment in judging if a particular comment was disrespectful, if the child understood the difference between

make-believe and a lie, or if the child's action was childish or destructive; but every such judgment call gives the parent opportunity to teach discernment and good decision making to their children.

3. Consequences must follow (as we will see in the next chapter).

To review, parents need to determine their boundary lines in advance. They must set them, teach them, and consistently enforce them through a variety of acceptable means. We have suggested the use of the 4 D's.

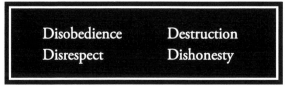

Disobedience   Destruction
Disrespect   Dishonesty

But whichever boundaries parents decide to establish, they must remember that children will **always** test the boundaries. Such testing is inevitable for three reasons:

1. The child's fallen nature prescribes that it will be so. *Isaiah 53:6a* teaches about this nature: "All we like sheep have gone astray; we have turned every one to his own way."

2. Children desire security, and finding out where the real boundaries are gives them that security. Security is one of the young child's driving needs; he or she will go to whatever means necessary to achieve it.

3. Children want this tangible evidence of a parent's love. Children who feel unloved are usually undisciplined children.

Chapter Five

Consequences

What son is he whom Father chasteneth not?
Hebrews 12:17b

One of a parent's main responsibilities in bringing up children is what I call "managing consequences." By this I mean that in every child's life, consequences will come—natural and manufactured consequences. Natural consequences are those that come naturally from behavior: a burn for touching something hot, a bad grade for not studying, or any variety of hurts for not being careful or wise in one's choices. Manufactured consequences are those that the parent institutes for teaching purposes, such as a spanking, a time-out, or some type of future restriction of a child's choices. The parents' job is to manage those consequences so that they are appropriate for the offense. Sometimes this may mean protecting a young child from natural consequences that could harm him for life, and sometimes it may mean manufacturing a consequence so that he will learn to obey.

Managing Consequences

1. Parents should limit the severity of natural consequences, especially when those consequences threaten the health and safety of the child, both now and in the future.

2. Parents should not eliminate all natural consequences, although "love" for the child may tempt the parent to try to do so. Real love will allow the child to learn from them. *Proverbs 13:24* gives an important guideline: "He that spareth his rod hateth his son: but he that loveth him chasteneth him quickly."

3. Consequences for choices are guaranteed by God. Some of His consequences may occur in the future (heaven or hell), some may occur immediately (gravity or heat), but they will all come. Therefore, a child must learn on small matters that consequences for wrong choices are certain, so he will not suffer from the consequences of wrong decisions on the important issues, such as deciding to accept or reject Jesus Christ as his personal Savior. The application of this is why the Scripture says, "Withhold not correction from the child: for if thou beatest him with the rod, he shall not die." (*Proverbs 23:13*)

4. Consequences should always be appropriate to the behavior. Consequences that are too severe for the offense generate anger in the child and oftentimes a desire for revenge. Consequences that are too small generate a lack of honor and encourage the bad behavior because the penalty is worth the pleasure of the actions.

5. Consequences should fit the behavior in the sense that the consequence is a direct outcome of wrong action. All consequences do not need to be a spanking. Spankings should be used primarily for the

four behaviors listed in chapter four, and other consequences should be used for desired character and good habit-forming behaviors. Homework not being done would be a common example. The consequences of not getting homework done would be that homework is always the first activity to be done after school, regardless of how much light is left in the day or what is going on in the child's world. The child's failure to do homework in the evening has caused him to lose his afternoon free time. The opposite can be true as well. If homework has been consistently done in the afternoon, the child can be given the option of choosing to do it in the evening as long as it is consistently getting done. An inappropriate consequence (see #4) would be for a child to lose a whole semester of afternoons for one missed homework assignment.

> **A child must learn that consequences for wrong choices are certain.**

Parents should start with a one-for-one approach, then possibly one week for one missed assignment, then loss of a month if the first plans do not work. Incremental escalation until the price becomes right for good choices is best used, but not so severe that good choices would never pay off.

6. Consequences should never involve any form of withdrawal of love, affection, or attention by the parent. A parent should remember that sometimes children do wrong in order to get attention, because of their need for the security of unconditional love.

Consequences such as being sent to their room should in some way be tied to the room (too messy, bed not made up) and not be used as a motive to "get this kid out of my hair" for awhile.

7. Consequences should never involve the putting down of the worth or value of the child, especially through the use of verbal put downs, ridicule, the calling of uncomplimentary names, or the over use of words like *always* or *never.*

Response to Consequences

Once a parent determines that the child's choice of behavior necessitates a manufactured consequence, he should keep in mind some important considerations in order for the consequences to be a form of training by discipline and not just a punishment for wrongdoing. Discipline and admonition both require consequences to be instructive and designed to limit such behavior choices in the future.

Parents can expect their children to respond to circumstances in one of two ways. Whether or not the consequences are natural or manufactured, their response will be either with an admission of guilt or a resistance to the rebuke.

Admission to Guilt—The admission of guilt will take two forms:

True Repentance—the child feels badly that he has hurt others or disobeyed his mother or father. He will accept the penalty as decided, with regret since he knows it will hurt him, but nevertheless he will accept it as just (if it is). He will ask for forgiveness; and when he fully understands the situation, he will make an effort to make restitution to those involved. This is an others-focused response.

There are times when admissions of guilt can be a little tricky because sometimes a child has learned to manipulate his parents into less discipline through an immediate admission of guilt. Such admissions are

48

usually insincere, and a parent must be vigilant of this behavior lest his efforts at correction be in vain. If the parent keeps his eyes open and knows that this is a possibility, the tactic is fairly easy to spot by the apparent anger or disbelief when the same punishment is metered out anyway. If leniency is given occasionally when it is warranted, a parent must be on guard at the next similar situation for the use of a quick admission of guilt as a way of manipulation. (Adults would probably do the same with a traffic officer if the last time they were pulled over they only received a warning instead of a ticket.)

True Regret—the child feels badly that he has been caught and must pay a penalty for his behavior choice.

> Consequences should never involve the putting down of the worth or value of the child.

He will inordinately focus on the consequences, just exactly what they are, how it will affect him, and often he will try to negotiate an alternate lesser penalty. There is little consideration of how his choice has affected others; his response is almost totally self-focused. The less mature the child is, the more likely his response will be a regret response. This is natural, especially in toddlers and very young children. Much teaching is required (admonition) to change their natural response of regret to a response of repentance.

This maturing process seems to follow other areas in life as well. Oftentimes in the Scripture the Lord addressed the crowds with warnings about avoiding hell (the rich man and Lazarus; *Luke 16:19–31*) and with admonitions to fear Him Who has the power of life and death and can send one to hell (*Luke 12:5*). Later in the epistles we learn what our sin has done to our Lord, how He has suffered for our sins, and how He has provided a salvation at a great price (*Philippians 2:1–11*). As we learn these things and mature in our Christian lives, we move from thinking about how all this affects me and start seeing how it affects a holy, loving, and yet just God. We mature from regretting our sins and looking to Jesus as an escape from hell, to a repentance that truly results in a change of direction and a focus on how our sin affects others, including our Lord.

Perhaps this explains why some people who are old in years but are not yet mature in their Christian lives are more concerned about what they can and cannot do as Christians than they are in how their behavior affects the cause of the One who died for them. They do not see the sacrifice of their personal rights as a reasonable service to their Savior (*Romans 12:1–2*).

The better parents are able to admonish their children in the difference between regret and repentance, the more prone the children will be to choose a life serving the Lord (no matter their occupation) rather than a totally self-centered life. A good character study on this is the difference between the sin of King Saul and his regret and the sin of King David and his repentance.

In the appendix of this booklet is a section entitled "Leading Your Child to Christ," which should be a help in deciding when and how parents should present the gospel to their children. The question is often asked, "When can a child be saved?" With proper instruction and without coercion, I believe it can happen at an early age. Perhaps the children's maturing to the point of understanding the difference between regret with a selfish view and repentance with an others view is an indicator of their readiness. We do know that the Lord in *Matthew 18* indicated that little children, small enough to be lifted in His arms, had the capacity of a humble faith that He said was necessary for anyone to be saved. He also implied that adults need to be careful that they do not despise the ability of these little ones to believe in Him.

Resistance to Rebuke—Resistance to rebuke will usually come in one of three different forms:

Blame Shifting—This is a diversion tactic as old as Adam and Eve, and both were guilty of using it. Mankind has followed suit ever since. The sooner parents can help their children understand that no one has the power to make them sin and that they must own up to their own shortfalls and mistakes, the sooner real repentance and confession can take place. Blaming others is attempting to change the parental focus in an effort to manipulate their parents away from themselves. Children can get amazingly creative at blaming other people, things, circumstances, and conditions. If parents fall for this ploy of misdirection, the children are dominating or manipulating them.

Denial—"I didn't do it," the bold lie, the half truth, the misdirection, the invention or modification of the facts—they are all attempts to evade the consequences of wrong behavior. A child's first real attempts at lying will often come in trying to evade responsibility and punishment. Sometimes parents will try to solve this one by just not pressing the issue or failing to ask probing questions. To do so is to place a monumental obstacle in the life path of their children.

Because Scripture says that all men are born liars at heart (*Romans 3:4*), and that Satan is the father of lies (*John 8:44*), parents need to be especially on guard to this tendency. Catching children at a lie is one of the best things parents can do for them. Parents should pray diligently to God for the wisdom and help to catch their children at every lie they try to tell. Whenever our children lied about their guilt and after they eventually admitted it, we would first chastise them for the misdeed, and then we would chastise them for the lie. We did this to emphasize how important the telling of truth was and what God thought of lies, as is indicated in *Proverbs 6:16–19* where God emphasizes His attitude with repetition: "These six *things* doth the LORD hate: yea, seven *are* an abomination unto him: A proud look, **a lying tongue**, and hands that shed innocent blood, A heart that deviseth wicked imaginations, feet that be swift in running to mischief, **A false witness *that* speaketh lies**, and he that soweth discord among brethren."

Rationalizing—This is an attempt to minimize the importance of the misdeed or to offer excuses that are designed to show it wasn't all that bad...besides...everyone else is doing it, too. The disobedience is now tolerable because it was such a small thing—"It was so little that I even forgot about it;" therefore, in the child's thinking it would be wrong for the parent to hold him accountable for the deed. Oftentimes, the child makes an attempt to put the guilt back on the parent, attempting again to deflect the consequences from himself. Rationalization is a sneaky little ploy and children can become very proficient at it if parents allow them to. Manipulation by rationalization is a tool that people of all ages use to redefine what God says is right and wrong and what He says about the only way of salvation. There are absolutes, and our children desperately need to learn those truths for the sake of their eternal destiny.

By remembering these three forms of resistance, parents can confront their children concerning wrong behaviors and easily spot and thus redirect a child's thought patterns toward admission of responsibility and repentance.

Chapter Six
The Use of Spanking as a Manufactured Consequence

The road and reproof give wisdom: but a child left to himself bringeth his mother to shame. Proverbs 29:15

Parents know there is no joy in administering a spanking. A parent's joy comes with the results of proper discipline and is spoken of in the Scriptures as the "peaceable fruit of righteousness." Spankings are just part of the whole process and should never be considered an act of discipline that stands alone. Proper and complete verbal teaching and training should always precede spanking.

How To Administer a Spanking—*Deuteronomy 8:5*

Pain is a defensive tool God has created within people to warn them that what they are doing is dangerous to their bodies or health. Pain can also be used as a training tool, a manufactured consequence, to help parents teach their children that certain forms of behavior are unacceptable and must be avoided. Parents must remember that the spanking is for the child's good, not the parents' satisfaction. A parent should never spank a child because it makes him feel good or relieves his frustrations. Spankings can be overused or out of control; a parent must be very careful to guard against these tendencies. The goal of spanking should be to help the child gain self-control of his will. Spanking is a humbling form of correction that, in essence, is an expression of parental love.

1. Parents must keep spankings objective in nature by determining ahead of time what they will spank their children for and never violate this list on the spur of the moment. When handled correctly and consistently, the child is then choosing when to get a spanking. The four D's of discipline in chapter four is the list Betty and I used with our children.

    *   Disobedience – to parents or authority

    *   Disrespect – verbal abuse of parents, other people, or God

    *   Destruction – willfully damaging property

    *   Dishonesty – deceit, lying, stealing, cheating, etc.

2. Parents must keep their cool and never lose their temper. If necessary, they should establish a waiting period to gain self-control (e.g., "Go to your room and wait for me.") If a parent struggles with self-control, he should use his spouse as a temperature gauge to establish when it is safe to proceed with the chastising.

3. Parents should explain the reason for the spanking first. Children need to admit their error or sin first. Ask them, "What did you do?" This questioning is an effective time to instruct them further so as to avoid future spankings. The following aspects should be reviewed:

    *   The communication of the command to be obeyed

    *   The choice they made and their understanding of their part

    *   The consequences that will come as a result

4. Parents must always spank their children in private. Maintaining the dignity of the child is important.

    •   No public slaps, spanks, or swats (*public* means in front of adults, other children, and siblings unless a situation should involve them).

    •   No bare skin—with the exception of taking off a diaper if the child is still in diapers.

    •   No screaming at the child, jerking him around, shaking him, or using other means to make him a public example.

5. Parents should never allow older children to struggle during a spanking. If children do struggle, more consequences should occur. For further illustration, see the "Suggested Procedures" section of this chapter.

    •   Struggling is an evidence of a lack of submission.

    •   Struggling is a manipulation tool to make parents pay too high a price to bother with a spanking the next time.

    •   Struggling can cause parents to lose their patience and can result in misplaced bruises.

6. Parents must be sure that the spanking hurts or stings, but never be damaging or abusive.

    •   Spankings that are not painful create bad attitudes.

    •   Most spankings should occur before age six, few between ages six and ten, and only on rare occasions for major infractions during adolescence. This is a parental decision and should be made with godly wisdom.

- The child should not be allowed to scream and yell; it is an act of rebellion. Crying is permissible for two to five minutes. If the crying or self-induced sobbing should continue, the child must know that he will receive more of the same if he does not stop. This would include attitudes of sulkiness and/or excessive sobbing.

- Spankings should be administered with a neutral, non-abusive object. The use of one's hand is unwise because children will identify the hand with punishment instead of love. This is seen when children flinch at the sudden approach of a parent's hand. A small paddle, as a ping pong paddle or a homemade one, will usually suffice. A parent bringing the paddle out and setting it on the table will oftentimes be a good warning signal to some children who are chastised by that particular paddle; other children will be impervious to its meaning. It is a way you can give your children a warning without even saying a word.

7. Parents should pray with their children (usually) and hold them tenderly after the spanking. Spending time with them at this time is never wasted but is vital to communicating the parents' unconditional love.

8. Soon after the spanking, parents must communicate to their children love and acceptance verbally and with actions. This should be done within thirty minutes; the children should not feel rejected. Parents should also be careful of falling into time and labor-consuming spanking procedures and traditions that, in the long run, may either discourage proper action or be used in some way to manipulate

a situation. For instance, some parents may avoid spanking a child because they believe they do not have quality time at that moment to spend with the child in properly teaching principles or in showing affection to the child after the spanking. What may be appropriate time spent for one situation may not be appropriate or necessary for the next.

9. Spanking our children is perceived as inappropriate to many in our country today, not because of its ineffectiveness, but because of misuse and abuse. Seen by some as harsh and unloving, many people believe spanking teaches children to be violent. These people do not have a proper understanding of the necessity to teach children obedience early in life through a proper and judicious use of manufactured consequences, including the biblically-correct use of spanking. Corporal punishment, as spankings, are actions of chastisement granted by God only to parents. Governments may have the God-given right of capital punishment, but not corporal punishment. Parents should therefore exercise great discernment in delegating to another adult the parental responsibility of corporal punishment.

10. Parents should not flaunt their use of spankings in front of others who may mistakenly perceive it to be harmful to the child. Those who disavow any use of corporal punishment usually also disavow the fact that God does now and will eventually hold everyone accountable for his own individual actions. Spankings should be designed to teach the reality of God's ultimate consequence—that even Jesus Christ had to pay the price for the sins of the whole world when He died upon the tree, and that was painful.

None of these principles or actions should be used to condone child beating or abuse.

Suggested Procedure for Spanking Used As Chastisement

1. **Have the child tell you why he is being punished.**

    Dad: "Billy, why does Daddy have to spank you?"

    Son: "I don't know."

    Dad: "Because you disobeyed Mommy."

    Dad: "Now why does Daddy have to spank you?"

    > **◄ Establish a disobeyed command that was properly communicated.**

    Son: "Because I didn't pick up my toys?"

    Dad: "No, Son, why does Daddy have to spank you?"

    Son: "Because I disobeyed Mommy."

    Dad: "What did Mommy tell you to do with your toys?"

    Son: "Pick them up when I was finished playing with them."

    Dad: "Were you finished playing with your toys?"

    Son: "Yes, sir."

    Dad: "Did you put your toys away?"

    Son: "No, sir."

    Dad: "Then did you disobey Mommy?"

    > **◄ Establish the child's choice to obey.**

    Son: "Yes, sir."

Dad: "What did Daddy
       and Mommy say
       would happen if
       you disobey?"

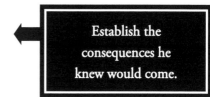

Establish the
consequences he
knew would come.

Son: "I would get a spanking."

Dad: "Then what does Daddy have to do?"

Son: "Spank me."

2. Tell him what his punishment is and how he is to handle it.

    Dad: "I'm going to give you some hard swats. If you kick,
           scream, fight me, or put your hands back there, you will
           get five more hard swats."

3. If he refuses to show repentance (if he is cocky or does not cry),
    repeat step two.

4. Following the spanking, let him cry it out for a short time; but do
    not let him sob and feel sorry for himself. Warn him that he will
    be spanked if he does not stop crying when he is told. He can
    stop, and he must if he is to learn self-control and benefit as God
    designed from the disciplining experience.

5. Assure him of your love and pray with him. You pray first and then
    have him pray. If he is too young, lead him in a prayer (a few words
    at a time).

    Dad: "Son, Daddy really loves you; that's why I want you to
           learn to do what is right and to learn that Jesus wants you
           to obey Mommy and Daddy. You pray now and tell Jesus
           you are sorry for disobeying Him and your mommy. Ask
           the Lord to forgive you and to help you obey."

6. **Do not leave him until he is restored.** Spend some time counseling, reassuring, and admonishing (teaching) him, especially in regards to proper restitution if others are involved.

7. At times it is appropriate to end with actions that show the relationship between parent and child has been restored. This can be done through touch (hugging and kissing, sitting on lap, etc.), by reading a story, or by playing or joking with him; don't leave him until you see evidence of an open and restored relationship with you.

   Dad: "What would you like to play, Son?"

   Son: "Let's play catch with the big green ball."

   Dad: "OK! Where is it? It looks like you ate it, Son! What should we do?"

   Son: "Daddy, you're being silly."

Reminder: Spanking is not synonymous with discipline; it is simply a tool or method used in discipline. In the Scriptures, the use of the Greek word *paideia* refers to corrective measures designed to eliminate those things in life that hinder growth. This word is most often used today as the word *discipline*, but it is translated as three different words in the New Testament (*Ephesians 6:4—nurture*; *2 Timothy 3:16—instruction*; *Hebrews 12:5, 7-9, 11—chastening*). All three of these words are the same word when translated, but each of them gives us a different aspect of discipline. True discipline training is a combination of all three. The translation of *paideia* as "chastening" is the closest application to spanking in the New Testament, but here again spanking is just one aspect of chastisement which can take on a variety of forms and methods.

Parents should not get stuck in the solo rut of spanking, but they must not neglect using this God-given tool in appropriate ways and for appropriate behavior choices. Spankings should not be used for such things as true unintentional accidents, bedwetting, potty training, or character development issues such as failure to do chores in a certain way or time frame. There are plenty of other consequences parents can manufacture for this type of behavior that better fit the offense. For older children who are still struggling with obedience, consequences can be agreed upon in advance between the parents and the children. Parents must be careful with this because the immaturity of youth will often suggest consequences that are inappropriate, too severe, or too lenient. Their suggestions will need to be mixed with a healthy dose of the parents' experience and maturity to be effective. The questions in the following box are starter points with older children when spanking is not wise.

Questions for Instructional Discipline

What did you do?
Not "why"; they have plenty of excuses

Was that right or wrong?
Teach values and judgment

How could you have handled this better?
Alternatives

Next time what will you do?
Agreement concerning future behavior

Should you fail, what would be a fair (just) punishment?
Establishes future consequences; be very consistent

Dangers To Avoid While Administering a Spanking

1. Threatening repeatedly without follow through

2. Acting in haste or in anger

3. Using a spanking as a punishment only—spanking does not equal disciplining.

4. Spanking for subjective and/or unclear reasons

5. Hitting or slapping your child on the hand, face, or head (in public or in private)

6. Thinking you can beat or spank a child into subjection—in the end, a child must freely choose to submit to authority in his life.

7. Waiting too long to administer a spanking—the younger the child, the closer to the offense the spanking must be to be effective. "Tomorrow is a new day" is a good motto to use.

8. Administering the spanking too hard or too soft—the spanking must hurt and sting, but not damage.

9. Using a spanking as the exclusive discipline tool or consequence

10. Using the spanking as a discipline tool too long into adolescence. Almost everything in a child's life changes after puberty; parents must change their tactics as well.

> If obedience issues have been handled wisely in earlier years, obedience should no longer be the main issue in the teen years; he should be a basically obedient, parent-honoring young person—not perfect, but growing.

Chapter Seven
The Work of Parenting

But we were gentle among you, even as a nurse cherisheth her children: For laboring night and day, because we would not be chargeable unto any of you, we preached unto you the gospel of God. Ye are witnesses, and God also, how holily and justly and unblameably we behaved ourselves among you that believe: as ye know how we exhorted and comforted and charge every one of you, as a father doth his children. 1 Thessalonians 2:7, 9b–11

Teaching children to obey is a process that sooner or later becomes hard work. This is true even though parents love their children, even though they keep the end goal in mind, and even though they have the help and encouragement of others. The process of setting clear and attainable expectations for the child clearly establishing consequences, applying a consistent standard (so something is not acceptable today and bad tomorrow), following through with appropriate and consistent consequences which include both chastisement for wrong doing and praise for doing right—is hard work. Accomplishing this work of parenting in an atmosphere of acceptance and love, while still exerting a strong *D factor* and thus communicating to the child who is in control, takes an enormous amount of energy and toil. Yet doing all this day by day, from birth until independence, becomes a labor of love that ultimately results not only in being good for the child but also in genuine joy and happiness for the parents.

Working at Parenting—A Labor of Love

Paul referred to such a labor of love, using the example of both a nursing mother and a cherishing father as models for his ministry in Thessalonica (*1 Thessalonians 2:7–11*). This night and day responsibility was motivated not only by affection and love but also by his desire to not be chargeable or responsible to them. This concept of not being responsible means that he did not want them to be able to honestly point back and say to him that if he had done better, they would have done better. Paul was saying he had done all he could; it was now up to them. But doing all he could meant a laboring (weariness in work) and travailing (painful work) night and day (constantly).

Hebrews 6:10–12 gives a little more insight into this kind of patience. Here the Scriptures are referring to those who diligently, through faith, labor for Him in love as doing so with patience. Patience, as defined in a word study dictionary, means "patience in respect to persons"; "forbearance, long–suffering, self–restraint before proceeding to action"… and is "associated with mercy and is used of God."[1] This is a labor so long and tedious that it can only be motivated by self-sacrificial love.

Few parents would argue with the description of parenting including the idea of work and labor. Yet few of them understood how much work parenting would be when they started to have a quiver full of children. There are three ingredients to what constitutes "work" that are applicable to parenting: initiative, industry, and tenacity.

Working at Parenting—The Need for Initiative

Initiative means that someone is a self-starter: he doesn't wait until some-one or something forces him to act. People with initiative are pro-active instead of reactive: they are thinking about needs and goals and figuring out the next step to take tomorrow while it is still today. When an em-ployer finds that kind of employee, he is indeed fortunate, as are the children of parents who take the initiative in their parenting responsibilities.

Children need parents who will discipline them on purpose rather than just on the spur of the moment, by chance, or because they are driving their parents crazy. But character traits, such as initiative, do not just turn on automatically when someone begins to have children. Abraham is a great biblical example of this type of parenting, and God recognized he would seize the initiative even before Isaac was born. Abraham was al-ready a person of initiative: he had already moved from Haran to Canaan at God's command.

God comes to Abraham with the news that He is about to judge Sodom and Gomorrah and asks Himself whether or not He should share His plans

> Children need parents who will discipline them on purpose.

with Abraham. He then answers Himself and decides to inform Abraham of His plans because Abraham will be the father of a great nation and be-cause in his own household he will "command his children...and they will keep the way of the Lord." Abraham's future child training affected God's present blessing on his family.

Genesis 18:18–19—Seeing that Abraham shall surely become a great and mighty nation and all the nations of the earth shall be blessed in him? For I know him, that he will command his children and his household after him, and they shall keep the way of the LORD, to do justice and judgment; that the LORD may bring upon Abraham that which he hath spoken of him.

This is the first passage in Scripture where the word *command* is used in relation to the rearing of children. It is from a Hebrew word that is used over 500 times in the Old Testament referring to one in authority giving orders to another under him. In this passage, the grammar indicates that it is happening now; but it is still looking toward the future as being an accomplished fact. This is interesting because God said it about one year before Isaac was born, but He could also observe Abraham's handling of his current stewardship responsibilities and project the same diligence into the future. The word *command* means "to constitute, to make firm, to establish, or to set in order… it is a picture of a superior giving verbal commands to a subordinate."[2]

However, the word *command* is used most often for commands that God is giving to mankind. The *Theological Wordbook of the Old Testament* gives some good insight concerning God's commands, and these are relevant to parents, because God's dealing with believers (His children) is an example of how parents are to deal with their children.

- "What God commands to be done, He provides the means to accomplish."

- "Blessing accompanies obedience to God's commands; rebellion, however, brings curses."

- God instructed Hezekiah…to make sure his responsibilities were…properly entrusted to his successors."

- "God clearly reveals His commandments in order that they be available to all the people." Thus, He gave the written word and the prophets.

- "To do the commands, man must remember them." Thus the use of visual reminders in the home, on clothing, and on jewelry were all to be accompanied by the teaching of the father as instructed in *Deuteronomy 6:6–9*.

- "The violation of any commandment results in guilt and the need for atonement."

- "The writer of Ecclesiastes searched every possibility for meaning to life and came to this conclusion: 'The end of the matter; all has been heard. Fear God, and keep his commandments; for this is the whole duty of man' (*Ecclesiastes 12:13*)."[3]

If parents were to apply these seven observations concerning the use of the word command to their upbringing responsibilities and word them as principles, they might go something like this.

Parents must take the initiative to:

- Make sure the commands they give to their child are "do-able" for the individual child. Parents must consider the physical and mental abilities and the current situation.

- Make sure they follow up their performance with immediate verbal praise or, if needed, corrective words giving further instructions and admonitions.

- Make sure they realize their training is for the long haul, intending for the children to learn to become independent of them.

- Make sure they teach what, how, and why, and follow with reminders and repetition as needed.

- Make sure they remember children are immature and are in the process of learning how to remember to do the next right thing. Chore lists, chore charts with pictures for the non-reader, posters, plaques around the home, notes left on refrigerators, or message board reminders are all helpful and a good step away from parents having to be present to give verbal commands in order for the child to obey. Deferred obedience with some reminders is a step of growth.

- Make sure consequences, both natural and manufactured, follow disobedience. They must be consistent and appropriate, and they must fit the offense. Parents must remember that because God's love sent Jesus to the cross to provide atonement for believers, parents should administer chastisement in love.

- Make sure they remember their goal. When children are small, their whole life revolves around their mother and father. As children mature, parents' desire should be that their children's first love and allegiance be transferred to God. Learning to obey parents helps children learn to obey God. The opposite is also true.

Working at Parenting—The Necessity for Guarding

Parents must guard themselves against unrealistic expectations. As parents are working at helping their child learn how to obey, the progress sometimes looks encouraging; and then there are times when it seems the child is going backwards at an alarming rate. My wife and I often wondered if everything we had taught our child had evaporated into thin air. The Lord graciously spared our family some needless agony by helping us to see the current situation in a clearer light.

Parents must remember that immaturity means that a child may often not maintain appropriate behavior when other

> God's dealing with believers is an example of how parents are to deal with their children.

things are interfering. The older a child gets, the more a parent can expect a child to act right, even when he does not feel right. But for the young child cutting his teeth, the whole world is a pain; and he does not mind letting everyone know that and may not respond to commands in the same loving way he did last week. This is not to say that the parent should tolerate disobedience; it is to say the parent needs to take the initiative to modify expectations and commands during this time. Some situations a parent may need to consider are health and security issues, including teething, over-tiredness, a new sibling, turmoil in the home, lack of routine, one parent away for a while, or distraction of a parent's attention because of work or personal problems. If life becomes a continual crisis, parents may need to make adjustments in their lifestyle.

Parents must also be on guard against phrasing a command as a question. If a parent says to his three year old, "Don't you want to go to bed now?" The child has every right to answer truthfully, "No!" So, if the parent really wants the child to go to bed now, he should phrase his command as such, "It is time to go to bed. Pick up your toys and let's get ready for bed." Parent should not give children an option to legitimately resist their command.

Parents must also be on guard for the passive rebel, the child who is never in trouble because he is never asked to do something he does not want to do. Or, he never says, "No," he just quietly drags his feet or does something really nice for his parent. But the bottom line is that he is not doing what he was told to do. A friend of our family once told us how she always got out of chores. When she was told to do a chore, she responded with, "I was just going to practice piano." She became a very good pianist, for her mother always fell for her ploy; but she regrets that she never learned to cook or clean or take care of needful responsibilities for her family.

Parents must not let down their guard when a child does just enough to get by. All children will try this manipulation ploy from time to time in order to get their parents off their back. The child will do part of what was asked, and parents are so relieved to see a little progress that they settle for incomplete obedience. For obedience to be real obedience, it must be complete obedience. Not only does complete obedience accomplish the whole task within the acceptable time frame but also it exemplifies an internal obedience. There is a difference between outward compliance and inward obedience. Noah Webster, when he published his first dictionary in 1828, defined obedience in a way that is still useful for us today. Webster was a great scholar, oftentimes researching roots to words in 26 different languages before assigning it a contemporary definition (for 1828). Because he knew that the everyday definition of words changed with usage, he tried to get to the root of the words to lay a foundation for understanding what the user of the word was really trying to say. Noah Webster was also a Christian; therefore, the majority of the words he had in his dictionary had references to the Bible usage and definition of that word. His dictionary is very useful for those of us who still use the King James Version as our everyday reading and study Bible. Webster implied that for obedience to be complete, and thus real, it had to include three things:

- a knowledge of what is required

- assent of the will to do what is required

- the doing of what is required

Keeping these three ideas in mind, a parent who wants his child to get up from the floor and sit in a chair will consider the child to be totally and inwardly obedient when three things take place: (1) the child hears and understands the command, (2) the child inwardly says, "Yes, I'll do that," and (3) the child does it.

- If the child fails to hear the command, but gets up and sits in the chair, obedience has not taken place.

- If the child hears the command but gets up and sits in the chair, inwardly fumes about the command, waits for the parent to turn his back and then returns to the floor, but then complies in order to avoid the consequences, real obedience has not taken place.

- If the child hears the command, inwardly accepts the command as a good thing to do, but then day dreams away the opportunity to do what is asked, obedience still has not taken place.

Obedience is much more than outward compliance. This is why the Scripture says to "bring them up in the nurture [discipline] and admonition [teaching] of the Lord." Discipline alone is not sufficient to bring them up in the Lord. Even in parenting, obedience is much more than outward compliance.

The last thing parents need to be on guard about is not to make too many excuses for disobedience. Notwithstanding what was written above concerning immaturity and expectations, parents must be careful not to fall into the trap of believing the disclaimers of many parents: "It's the sugar, it's in their genes, they're tired, he's ADHD, his father was the same way," and so on.

Conclusion

Thus, we conclude that the responsibility of parenting is work and requires one to be constantly on guard. Always being on duty is hard, but that is why the Apostle Paul referred to parenting as a labor of love. This kind of love is *agape* love, a self-sacrificing love for our children, and it comes with a cost. The cost for such love is diligent work and constant vigilance. Disciplining, training, and teaching our children in a God-honoring way is not easy; but it is God's established method of bringing up children to choose God's way and to then teach their own children to do likewise.

1. Zodhiates, Spiros. *The Complete Word Study Dictionary New Testament.* Chattanooga, Tennessee: AMG Publishers, 1992, page 939.
2. Zodhiates, Spiros. *The Complete Word Study Old Testament.* Chattanooga, Tennessee: AMG Publishers, 1994, page 2358.
3. Harris, Archer, and Walke. *The Theological Wordbook of the Old Testament, Volume 2.* Chicago: Moody Press, 1980, pages 757–758.

Chapter Eight
Bottom Line Principles

Behold to obey is better than sacrifice. 1 Samuel 15:22b

Principle One: The foundation of the family is obedience.

The first question to be asked and answered in the family is, "Who is in control?" The right answer is that ultimately God is in control. Parents obey God through obedience to the Scriptures; then children obey parents in the home. The parents' example is the key to children really learning who is in control in the family. Parents undermine the authority of God when they do not obey God in requiring their children to obey them.

Mom proves that God is in control by lovingly submitting to the leadership of her husband in the family. Dad proves to his children that God is in control by exercising the loving leadership, including teaching and leading in spiritual things, in the family. When Christian parents have children who comply on the outside but inwardly are rebellious, they need to focus first on this issue of disobedience relating to the biblical roles in the home as the underlying cause. Are parents really willing, internally, to "do family" according to God's Word? *Luke 6:46–49* tells the parent what happens when a family knows the Bible but has failed to build their family upon its truths through obedience to God's Word. When trouble comes, this disobedient family falls. The foundation of the Christian family is obedience.

Principle Two: Delayed discipline is disastrous.

Proverbs 13:24 says that "He that spareth his rod hateth his son: but he that loveth him chasteneth him betimes." The root definition of the word *betimes* goes back to the old agrarian ways of doing one's chores. The idea was to get up at dawn or before dawn and diligently go about accomplishing the task. *Strong's* dictionary says it means to "seek, diligently, early in the morning." My belief is that 90% of the discipline chores of parents should be accomplished by the age of five. It is not that a parent cannot wait until later or that he cannot be successful if he has waited until later. The problem is that the longer the parent waits, the harder it becomes for the child to submit his will, in humility, to his parents, his other authorities, and ultimately to God. Notwithstanding, wherever a parent is on the child-rearing journey, teaching obedience is the first and most crucial step. The obedience step must still be taken even if the child is over the five-year mark, over the ten-year mark, or even into the teen years. This is not a step that can be skipped altogether.

Some parents may say, "I'll wait until he is ready to learn, until I'm sure he can understand what I'm saying." Some parents have a strong enough *D factor* to do that and succeed, but I feel sorry for them because this delay transforms the glorious years of youth into a struggle for control, a struggle that could have been won much easier in the preschool years. I have a friend in the camp ministry who was a horse trainer by trade before going into the ministry. One time many years ago someone wanted to donate a horse to Ironwood. The horse had great blood lines, was mature, and not old—just right for our horsemanship program. I asked my friend Rick to go with me to see the horse. The horse was a mare with great conformation, but she was totally unbroken. No one had taught her to yield to man, to yield to pressure, to submit to a rope. We had to sadly leave her behind because she was unfit for our purposes. Some may say such a horse could be broken to ride. That may be true, but at what price? I remember Rick saying someone could really get hurt with that horse, and we would never really know for sure if she would ever be usable with youth in our camp program. No doubt, someone could find a use for her, but not us. Working with rebellious, defiant teenagers is a little like that mare. It can be done, maybe, but they are much too big and too strong for parents to use force on; the young person must be willing to submit. The choice is theirs. How much easier it is to start when the children are young. We have young people gentling and handling young horses that have never been ridden before; but we start the horse in the gentling process when they are just months old—getting used to being handled, learning what a rope is, learning to give or yield to pressure from that rope or from people. In this way, a young person of only a hundred or so pounds can train a horse weighing over 1000 pounds. But in order to do that, he must start with the horse *betimes,* when the horse is just months old.

New parents don't realize how intelligent the little newborn is because the baby is not talking immediately and is so helpless physically. Most children will be talking by the time they are two. While I studied Spanish for three years in high school and college, I still have trouble saying "howdy" in Spanish. A child will learn half of everything he will ever learn in his life by age ten. Yet many parents believe they can house-train a six-month-old puppy better than they can teach their six-month-old child to respond to "no" in an appropriate fashion. That child is much more intelligent and capable of great learning than the dog is. Chapter nine in my book, *Dangerous Parenting Detours*, deals with this subject of delayed discipline in greater detail.

Principle Three: The desired product demands a definite process.

The desired product is children receiving Christ's free gift of salvation, growing into mature young men and women, personally making choices to honor God first in their lives, loving and honoring their parents even as they leave home to wed another believer and establish their own Christian home, being pure as they go to the altar that glorious day, and continuing to desire to walk worthy of God.

If that is the desired end product, parents must go through the process to get there. They must remember, "No process; no product." In the first chapter we said, "No shortcuts!" In essence, we are just repeating that principle here. There are a number of steps in the process to that desired end product. After the essential process of keeping the relationship between the parents biblically sound, the first real step with the child is the absolutely necessary step of learning to obey!

To put this principle into practice, the parent must first have a definite goal in mind. Parents must start by thinking through what they want their children to be like when they are grown and on their own. Writing down those descriptions helps to solidify and evaluate the parents' thoughts; selecting a verse from the Scriptures that summarizes that goal

> The desired product is children receiving Christ's free gift of salvation, growing into mature young men and women, personally making choices to honor God first in their lives, loving and honoring their parents even as they leave home to wed another believer and establish their own Christian home, being pure as they go to the altar that glorious day, and continuing to desire to walk worthy of God.

helps to keep the goals biblical. A few suggestions as such possible key verses might be the following:

- *Luke 2:52*
- *1 Thessalonians 2:12*
- *Colossians 1 :28–29*
- *1 Timothy 3:17*
- *Romans 12:1–2*

Each child is different; he is a unique creation of God. As such, parents will not be able to treat each child exactly alike. Parents should adapt the principles in this book to each of their children, designing a unique program or process for each child within the guidelines of the same unchanging, absolute truth of the Word of God.

Principle Four: Parents must establish an environment of security without selfishness.

If parents are desirous of an environment of security in the family, unconditional love is the bottom-line attitude that must pervade the family. This unconditional love does not have to be earned; it is the kind of love

83

God has for believers, the love that guarantees our eternal security as believers. We may sin; but we are still saints, blood-bought children of God, eternally secure in Him. What a wonderful truth that is! Parents teach this truth about God to their children by ensuring that their love for them is not contingent upon the child's performance or obedience. Such receiving of unconditional love gives security, but such an exalted position can lead to pride and "me-firstism."

To combat that possible arrogance, the Lord has told His children to first love Him with a self-sacrificing love, and then to love others. When we become believers, we are born into the family of God not only as sons but also as servants of others. Lessening the natural selfishness in children requires teaching and discipline; the parent's goal is that the child would decide to put others first as his service to God, sacrificing for others as Christ did for him. Mom and Dad can be powerful examples as they are teaching this principle to their children. Children will not be allowed to do certain things but will be required to do other things for the good of others. Parents must decide to take the time to teach the "whys" of certain actions—because others come first. The process of learning delayed gratification is a great tool in teaching this principle. The child can be taught to wait until the right time, starting with the right time to eat, getting desserts, playing, and staying up later. As they learn to wait for others and learn the right time and place for activities, they learn an invaluable lesson of placing others first.

For a child, security results in knowing where the boundaries are. They are smart enough to know where the parent's boundaries are, even if the parent does not know. Whether it is the tenth time or the thirtieth time the parent told the child to pick up his toys, the child knows the tone of voice that means to do it now or pay a price that is too high. Many times, unknown to the parent, the child picks up on certain signals. How much

> For a child, security results in knowing where the boundaries are.

better it would be if the child didn't have to resort to such a subjective method. Parents must learn to be consistent with their words in a normal tone of voice, not repeating the command or raising the volume.

A parent simply needs to decide how many times he wants to tell his child to do something before the child obeys. If the parent wants to give every command to his child five times before the child obeys, he should in a normal tone tell the child five times and then spank the child for disobedience. After the parent does so in a consistent manner, the child will learn the pattern and conform to it—five warnings means a spanking; so, he will wait until the fourth time and then obey. If the parent wants to only say something once, he should say it once and then spank if the child does not obey. The child will learn the same pattern and be secure. Children become insecure when the parent gives a spanking after a one-time command today, after a five-time command tomorrow, after a three-time command the next day, and then back to a one-time command. Inconsistency leads to a child's insecurity and will eventually generate fear and, sooner or later, anger.

When considering the security of children in the home, the relationship of the parents is of the utmost importance. It is absolutely impossible for a child to be secure and happy if he has any suspicions that "Mommy and Daddy don't love each other." Hearing the words is good, but seeing the evidence of love is absolutely essential.

Principle Five: Honor all men.

Children are commanded by God to honor their parents in *Ephesians 6:2–3:*

> Honour thy father and mother; (which is the first command-
> ment with promise;) that it may be well with thee, and thou
> mayest live long on the earth.

Fathers are commanded to honor mothers in *1 Peter 3:7:*

> Likewise, ye husbands, dwell with them according to knowl-
> edge, giving honor unto the wife, as unto the weaker vessel, and
> as being heirs together of the grace of life; that your prayers be
> not hindered.

Mothers are commanded to honor fathers in *Ephesians 5:32–33:*

> This is a great mystery: but I speak concerning Christ and the
> church. Nevertheless let every one of you in particular so love his
> wife even as himself; and the wife see that she reverence (honor)
> her husband.

Parents are commanded to honor children (as all men) in *Romans 12:10:*

> Be kindly affectioned one to another with brotherly love; in
> honor preferring one another.

The command to children to honor their parents was the first command
in the Ten Commandments that dealt with man's relationship with man
and is, without a doubt, one of the primary foundational principles of
the family. God wants His people to respect one another (*1 Peter 2:17*).
Respect and honor for one another recognizes the other person as a

unique creation of God; respecting each other honors God. Respect is a key element in the formation of true and lasting relationships.

A parent fails to honor his child when he fails in his disciplining responsibilities, but he also dishonors his child when he fails to treat the child differently as the child matures and grows. The total control a parent has over the child's life at birth must be gradually relinquished as the child matures in life. This relinquishing of control is very difficult for some parents and thus creates conflicts with their children that will cloud the relationship for years to come. It is a matter of respecting God's way and respecting that new emerging adult growing in the home. Whole books have been written on this one subject, but it is probably not that complicated. A parent needs to mentally put himself in the other person's place and treat him the way he would want to be treated.

My wife and I have been on the wonderful receiving end of God's grace in relation to our children. We were simple enough in our Christian belief and faith that we just believed what the Bible said and did it. We call that obedience to God, but it is based on our belief on a good and loving God Who sent His own Son Jesus Christ to the earth and the cross to pay a substitutionary price for our sins to be forgiven and for our adoption into the family of God for eternity. This free gift of salvation is offered

To sinners—For all have sinned, and come short of the glory of God. (*Romans 3:23*)

In love—But God commendeth his love toward us, in that, while we were yet sinners, Christ died for us. (*Romans 5:8*)

And given freely to all who believe— That if thou shalt confess with thy mouth the Lord Jesus, and shalt believe in thine heart that God hath raised him from the dead, thou shalt be saved. For with the heart man believeth unto righteousness; and with the mouth confession is made unto salvation. (*Romans 10:9–10*) Some may want to verbalize their faith by calling on the Lord for forgiveness and salvation. His instruction is clear—For whosoever shall call upon the name of the Lord shall be saved. *(Romans 10:13)*

Just as Betty and I believed God and His Word for salvation, we also believed that such a God would clearly give us instructions on how best to rear the children He loves and died for. May God help us all to obey Him by faith as we teach our children to obey.

Provoke Not Your Children to Wrath
Self-Study Worksheet

And ye fathers, provoke not your children to wrath: but
bring them up in the nurture and admonition of the Lord.
Ephesians 6:4

Fathers, provoke not your children to anger, lest they be discouraged.
Colossians 3:21

1. Anger is _____ — *Ecclesiastes 7:9;*
    Matthew 5:22; Romans 12:19

2. Anger is considered by God to be a work of the _____.
    Galatians 2:20

3. Anger is a characteristic of _____. *Proverbs 12:16; 14:29*

4. Anger is connected with:

    a. _____ *Proverbs 21:24*

    b. _____ *Genesis 49:7; Proverbs 27:3–4*

    c. _____ *Ephesians 4:31*

    d. _____ *Colossians 3:8*

    e. _____ *Proverbs 21:19; 29:22*

5. Anger may be averted by:

    a. A soft _____ *Proverbs 15:1*

    b. _____ *Proverbs 29:8; Proverbs 13:10*

6. Anger should be considered in the choice of _____. *Proverbs 22:24*

7. Anger destroys _____. *Proverbs 18:19*

8. Anger has _____ at its root. *Proverbs 13:10; James 3:14*

9. The causes of anger are: (as illustrated in *Numbers 20:1–13*)

    a. Fear

    b. Frustration

    c. Hurt/loss

10. Anger may be evidenced by the following. Mark the three ways that you most likely express your anger.

    ☐ Demands

    ☐ Distortion

    ☐ Displeasure

    ☐ Destruction

    ☐ Repression

    ☐ Suppression

    ☐ Expression

    ☐ Confession

Answers: 1. forbidden, 2. flesh, 3. fools, 4a. pride, b. cruelty, c. bitterness, clamour, evil-speaking, d. blasphemy, e. strife and contention, 5a. answer, b. wisdom , 6. friends, 7. families/relationships, 8. pride

What Provokes

A survey taken among middle-year teens yielded the following list of ways parents provoke their children to wrath.

Parents:

1. Are not consistent with rules, discipline, etc.

2. Don't let "us do what we want"

3. Are hypocritical; have a double standard

4. Have a closed mind; no opportunity to really discuss things

5. Don't let us grow up—no independence

6. Don't believe in us; don't trust us

7. Don't respect us—respect is only a one-way street

8. Won't let us give our side of the story

9. Nag us

10. Aren't satisfied—what I've done is never good enough

11. Keep bringing up the past

12. Ignore us when we are talking

13. Play favorites

14. Embarrass us by their husband/wife relationship

15. Don't spend time with us; won't listen

16. Use our dependence on us like a club

17. Want us to serve them, but they don't want to serve us

18. Don't respect my privacy

19. Want me to be a "super student"

20. Make fun of me or discipline me in public

Survey taken by Walt Brock. Ironwood Christian Academy, 1995.

Appendix B

Leading Your Child to Christ
The *Wordless Book*

And said, Verily I say unto you, Except ye be converted, and
become as little children, ye shall not enter into the
kingdom of heaven. Matthew 18:3

The *Wordless Book* has been used for many years in explaining the gospel to children. Below is a clear and simple approach to lead your child to a saving faith in Jesus Christ. Ask questions to see if he understands. If he does not understand, do not tell him the answer you want. Use the time as a teaching time. If the child will not readily admit he is a sinner, explain what the Scriptures say about his being a sinner, but do not try to lead him to Christ at this time. Explain to him that you will talk another time and will keep learning what the Bible says. Do not ever put pressure on the young child to repeat the sinner's prayer; nor should you allow siblings to apply pressure. Teach the siblings to pray and be a good example without applying pressure. After saying all of this, I urge you to remember that Christ told us to come to Him as a little child—-with the same wonder and simple faith as one of these little ones.

Luke 18:17—Verily I say unto you, Whosoever shall not receive
the kingdom of God as a little child shall in no wise enter therein.

Even if you use the *Wordless Book* to visually present the gospel and even if your child cannot read, have your Bible open to *John 3:16*.

The Gold Page (Experience has proved it is wise to begin with the gold page, stressing the love of God.)

The story begins on the gold page. It reminds me of the street of gold in heaven that the Bible talks about. Do you know who lives in heaven?

God does and He wants you to be in heaven with Him some day.

You usually like to be with people you love, don't you? That's why God wants you to be with Him in heaven—He loves you very much! In the Bible, God's Word, He says, "I have loved thee with an everlasting love." (*Jeremiah 31:3*) That means that God loved you even before you were born! You could put your name in there and say, "God has loved me with an everlasting love," and it would be just as true.

What does *John 3:16* say about God's love?

God wants you to be in heaven someday with Him, *but there is something that can keep you from being there—sin.*

The Dark Page (Use this page to stress the spiritual need of the child. As you talk about sin, pray that the Holy Spirit will bring conviction.)

This dark page reminds me of the darkness of sin.

Sin is the bad things that people do. It is anything that you do or say or think or even feel that is against God. It is things like lying, cheating, disobeying your parents, fighting with brothers or sisters, or not being kind to someone.

The Bible says that everyone has sinned; it plainly says, "for all have sinned" (*Romans 3:23*). When the Bible says, "all have sinned," that includes both you and me, too, doesn't it?

Yes, you and I and everybody else in the whole world have sinned and done wrong things. The Bible says you and I were born with a kind of "want to" to do wrong. Your mother didn't have to teach you how to disobey, did she? Neither did mine.

You probably get punished for doing wrong things at home, don't you? Those are the kinds of things God calls sin. God has a punishment for sin. It is to be separated from Him forever in a place of punishment the Bible calls hell. But God doesn't want you to go there. That is what *John 3:16* means when it says that some people will "perish"—that they will go to hell forever.

Remember, He loves you and wants you to be in heaven with Him someday. In fact, He wants to be your Heavenly Father right now.

But if I were to end the story right now it would seem like no one is going to heaven. Because God will not allow sin in heaven and everyone has sinned! *But God made a way for the problem of sin to be taken care of.*

The *red page* tells about that.

The Red Page (Use this page to stress the way of salvation through the death of Christ.)

Jesus is God's perfect Son; He is God the Son. That means that He is God and He became a man and lived a perfect life. The Lord Jesus was the only person in all of history to ever live His entire life without sinning.

You would think that everyone would love someone like that, and yet when He grew up, wicked men took the Lord Jesus and nailed Him to a wooden cross. This red page reminds me that they left Him there to bleed and die.

When He died He was taking the punishment for something He didn't even do. He was willingly taking the punishment for every sin that you and I and everyone in the world has ever done. The punishment was to die. And the Lord Jesus knew that the only way that your sin could be forgiven would be if *He* would die for you. ***Jesus died for your sins.*** The Bible says that "without shedding of blood is no [forgiveness]." (*Hebrews 9:22b*) When *John 3:16* says that God gave His only Son, He was talking about Jesus dying on the cross for our sins.

As He died, the Lord Jesus said, "It is finished." Everything that needed to be done for your sins to be taken away had been done by Him on the cross.

They buried His body. But three days later He proved that He could take away your sins and give you everlasting life by coming back to life! And without dying again, He returned to heaven, where He is today.

Because Jesus is God's Son who died for you, you can become His child right now!

The *clean page* (white page) tells how.

The Clean Page (Use this page to stress the child's part—to believe on the Lord Jesus as his personal Savior.)

You remember that God loves you so much and wants to be your Heavenly Father and have you live with Him in heaven someday. But your sin separates you from Him. That's why He sent His Son, the Lord Jesus to die on the cross for you.

The Bible says, "But as many as *received* Him (the Lord Jesus), to them gave He power to become the sons of God, even to them that *believe* on His name." (*John 1:12*) That means that if you *believe* with all your heart that Jesus died for you and rose again and *receive* Him by inviting Him to come and take away your sins, He will make you a part of God's forever family—God will become your Heavenly Father right now, and someday you will share God's home with Him in Heaven. *John 3:16* says if we believe in Him we will have everlasting life in heaven with Him.

Have you ever believed and received the Lord Jesus so you could become God's child?

I'm not talking about whether you attend church or have been baptized or if your parents are Christians. Those things are good, but they cannot take away even one sin. He wants *you* to believe and receive Him.

If you believe that Jesus, God's Son died for *your* sins on the cross and rose again, would you tell God right now:

1. *that you know you have sinned.*
2. *that you believe Jesus, God's Son, died for you and rose again.*

3.   *that you are inviting Him to be your Savior and your Heavenly Father.*

You could pray something like this:

Dear God, I know that I have sinned and done wrong against you. I believe that Jesus is God's Son and that He took the punishment for all my sins by dying on the cross. I believe He came back to life again. I receive you now as my only Savior from sin. Thank you for making me your child right now as you promised. In Jesus' name, amen.

If you really prayed these words and meant it, God has just made you a part of His forever family! It's not because I said so, but because He promised (remember *John 1:12*?); and God never breaks His promises.

Let me show you another great promise for you in God's Word. *Hebrews 13:5* says, (God is speaking) "I will never leave thee, nor forsake thee." Will the Lord Jesus ever leave you? He promises, "No." How about if you sin again? No, God says, "**I will never leave you.**" And *Hebrews 13:6* says, "The Lord is my helper." He will give you the power to do what is right.

When you become God's child, He wants you to grow to know Him better each day.

The last page, the *green page*, tells you how.

The Green Page (Stress spiritual growth on this page.)

Green reminds me of things that grow. (Like trees and grass and plants.) When you become God's child, He wants you to get to know Him better—to grow in how well you know Him (*2 Peter 3:18*).

Sin can keep that from happening. But God promises in *I John 1:9*, "If we confess our sins, He is faithful and just to forgive us our sins and to cleanse us from all unrighteousness." That means that if you sin you need to confess (tell on yourself) to God. "He is faithful" means He will always forgive you. And "just" means that God is fair to forgive you because He already punished every sin you've ever done when Jesus died for you on the cross.

You can get to know God better by reading and obeying His Word, the Bible. Another thing that can help you grow in God is by talking to God in prayer. Going to a church and Sunday school that teach from the Bible will help you know Him better, too.

You can also tell others about Jesus! In fact, If you have just become God's child right now, would you let me know? I would like to thank God for what He has just done for you. It would be a good idea for you to thank Him right now as well.

That Little Book

It's been around a long time now—well over a hundred years. That little *Wordless Book*. Whose brain-child was it? When did it first make an appearance?

"Give me 26 lead soldiers and I will conquer the world," exclaimed Benjamin Franklin. He referred, of course, to the alphabet from which he could form words and sentences, print a newspaper, and produce a book. But the *Wordless Book* conquers without any words. It speaks through the universal language of color.

That little book started with but three pages—black, red and white. In 1866, at the Metropolitan Tabernacle in London, Charles Spurgeon preached a sermon entitled the *Wordless Book*. In it he told of an old unnamed minister who had put three pages together and often looked at them to remind himself of his sinfulness, of Christ's blood poured out for him, and the cleansing provided. Spurgeon then said, "I want you, dear friends, to read this book this evening....may God the Holy Spirit help us do so to our profit."

When was the gold page added? We do not know, but it brought another dimension to the book, depicting the glories of heaven. We do know it was there nine years later when D. L. Moody used it. In the biography written by his son, William R. Moody, and published in 1900, he records:

One of the most interesting meetings at Liverpool (January/February 1875) was the children's service, where Mr. Moody and Mr. Sankey were both present. Some of the papers put down the number in the Victoria Hall at twelve thousand, with an overflow meeting of about two thousand in the Henglers Circus. Mr. Moody gave an address founded on a book with four leaves, black, red, white and gold, a sort of running inter-change of simple yet searching questions and answers. Responses were very promptly given.

Who hasn't heard of blind Fanny Crosby, the author of "Blessed Assurance," "Saved by Grace," and hundreds more old hymns? Fanny loved children. "Tell us a story, Fanny. Tell us another," they begged. Fanny would take from her purse a *Wordless Book* and tell them the story of which they never tired.

In 1895, the book traveled to India with Amy Carmichael. In Elisabeth Elliot's recent biography of her, *A Chance to Die*, she tells how Amy and her helper made a satin flag of gold, black, red, and white, hoisted it in the cart pulled by oxen and went from village to village in southern India telling the Gospel. "A most useful text for an impromptu sermon," Amy commented. In smaller groups she used the little book itself.

My first acquaintance with the book came in 1924. "Look what I found at the Bible bookstore," a fellow-student exuded as she burst into our training class one morning. "It will be great to show the boys and girls the way of salvation and lead them to Christ." The bookstore was operated by Dr. Harry A. Ironside before he became pastor of Moody Memorial Church in Chicago. The book was published by Pickering and Ingles in London.

When Child Evangelism Fellowship began to print that little book 15 years later, they added the final color, green, to represent Christian growth. They also published a leaflet telling how to use the book and giving Scripture verses for each page. In the ensuing years the message has been taken to over 80 countries by missionaries to boys and girls. Thousands of national workers have been taught how to use the *Wordless Book* with their own children.

Excerpts taken from Child Evangelism Fellowship Inc. and Ruth Overholtzer, PO Box 348, Warrenton, MO, 63383 / (636) 456-4321 and Berean Bible Ministries, goodnews@berean.org.